At the Edge

Melodramatic
A ^ Comedy

Jennifer DiMarco

Other books in print by Jennifer DiMarco:
*Escape to the Wind
Fall Through the Sky

*not published by Pride

At the Edge
copyright 1993 by Jennifer DiMarco
published by Pride Publications

ISBN 1-886383-11-1

First edition August 1994.
Second revised edition January 1997.
9 8 7 6 5 4 3

Cover art by Chris Storm.
Interior and cover design by Pride Publications.

All facts contained in this work were accurate as of 8/94.

Printed in the United States of America.

For a courageous woman
Chris Anne Wolfe
who, dying,
helped teach me to live

For the man in my memories
and the faded photographs
my father, Jared Landis Emond,
who died to protect me

For the little sister I was smart enough to ask for
and lucky enough to get
Angela Marie DiMarco
whose talent brought this play to life

Author's Introduction

Chris Anne entered my life with the magic of the Goddess in her deep-sea-shadow eyes and silver curls. She brought with her a love for life so strong that my entire outlook was changed. Her sense of humor, both light and dark, and her passion for words have become part of my heart. We met when I was on a book tour, and I will always remember looking up from my autographing, meeting her gaze... and spelling my name wrong.

In December of 1990, Chris Anne was diagnosed as a 4B with Hodgkin's Lymphogranuloma. Cancer. In September, 1993, the doctors announced that she had eighteen months to live. In September, 1996 she took her twentieth trip to Disney Land. But despite everything, the fact remains that there is no cure. She has undergone all possible treatments and has not held remission. She insists that she is not living with cancer; she is dying of cancer. With courage and with pride, she is dying.

Jared was young man with long, dark hair and a fierce protective nature. He was soft-spoken with a gentle smile, loving to write and draw. He was also very afraid of death and dying. Maybe because life hadn't given him all his answers yet. He is the first person I remember seeing cry.

I have never publicly spoken about my father before this. I have published numerous articles and stories about the parents who raised me – my Mama and my Mumu – but I have not told the story of my father who "disappeared" when I was not quite five years old. I can only imagine that this silence must seem like shame or disinterest on my part, but it is not. I am very proud of my father and embrace his place in my heart and my life.

I would like to tell his story now. I would like the world to know how brave my father was. But at twenty-five years old, he found himself in danger, in fear of his life. On a crisp autumn day he gathered the family together and pleaded that if something were to happen to him we would do nothing because it would only endanger the life of his daughter and he would not have that. Not ever. After that day he was never seen or heard from again. His body was never found. Nothing can be done. Perhaps even these few words are too much.

I cannot do what I want to do. I cannot heal Chris Anne. I cannot bring my father back. But I learned very early that there is one thing I can always do. I can write. This play is for them and, in some ways, even about them.

Character List

Therese Weaver

Daniel O'Donald

Television
Radio
Panhandler
Prostitute
Pusher
Realties 1 - 6

Cast Descriptions

Therese is a published poet. She wears her hair long, favoring blouses and slacks. Ever since she was a child, death has been part of her life as she loses loved ones. She believes that death constantly looms over life and she is always searching for that one thing that may be stronger than death – something, anything that would make life worth all the trouble of living. The recent death of Therese's mother has pushed Therese over the edge and she is consumed with dark thoughts. Therese tends to be melodramatic, never realizing how ridiculous she can be when she gets like this.

Daniel owns her own construction company and is a political activist. She is also HIV+. Daniel wears her hair short and favors jeans, works boots and sleeveless tee-shirts. She always wears a red ribbon pinned to her shirt. Brave and out-spoken, Daniel has a sometimes sarcastic sense of humor. She has found great freedom by accepting death as part of life and by embracing the reality of death in her own life. However, Daniel has not been able to over-come a fear of touch. She avoids physical contact with everyone because this is the one fear – illogical as it may be – that she cannot face.

The Voices. Though the play is essentially a two-woman play, there are several off-stage voices and announcers that are heard throughout the production. These voices can be male and/or female but are always ominous and powerful – harsh reality intruding into Therese and Daniel's world. The voices include the **Television**, the **Radio**, the **Panhandler**, the **Prostitute** and the **Pusher**. In addition, there are six times that announcements are heard. I call these the **Realties** and I suggest that the lines be taken by six different speakers if possible.

Main Set Descriptions

Overall, sets for "At the Edge" are simple. The power of the production rests in the hands of the actors themselves and the lighting.

Therese's House: Therese's house is in the center of the stage but set back behind the curtain line. This allows the house to remain intact even when action takes place in front of it – the curtain can be drawn to hide the house. However, the house should be set up on a platform to aid visibility. A table and a desk sit in the front – the desk with a typewriter surrounded by crumbled papers and the table with a cutting block and knife. Set back from the table is a counter with drawers, two mugs, a coffee pot and a microwave. Set back from the desk are two pillars where the Television and the Radio sit. They should stand just a few inches above Therese's head. An outside door opens into the kitchen area.

Daniel's Framework: The framework resembles a scaffolding – a ten foot tall rectangular metal or wood frame with a few crossbeams connecting the corner posts and a wooded platform built about half way up. Another platform, only half as large as the first, is built two feet higher than the first, creating a shelf-like ledge. There are buckets of nails, sanding blocks, hammers and a few other tools scattered around on the stage below the framework and on the platforms. The framework stands to one side of the stage and is set close to the front. It can remain on stage throughout the production or be pulled off when not in use.

The Edge Cafe: The cafe is set up in such a way that it is completely mobile. This is to accommodate action that takes place before and after the cafe scenes that requires use of the entire stage. The cafe consists of a hanging sign, one table covered with a table cloth, two chairs and one large, leafy plant – probably a Dracaena Massangeana, or "Corn Plant."

Author's Acknowledgements

First, I'd like to thank the readers from all over the world who are disproving the stereotype that stageplays don't sell. I look forward to third, fourth and even tenth editions of "At the Edge" because of the precedent they continue to set.

I would also like to thank Cris Newport and Angela DiMarco. Cris is, without a doubt, the best editor a writer could ever have; she is patient, fair and incredibly concise. And with her expertise in technical theater, her lighting suggestions were vital to the evolution of this play.

Last, but never least, my sister, Angel, was the first to bring "At the Edge" to life with her phenomenal performance of Daniel's monologue from Act Two, Scene Two. Her dynamic talent has always been obvious but the passion, pain and humanity she brought to Daniel that day will be part of me forever.

Thank you – all of you – for making this, the fully revised second edition of "At the Edge," possible. I couldn't have done it without you.

At the Edge

Edge

Comedic

A ^ Melodrama

Jennifer DiMarco

Act One

Two Paths Meet

Scene One

Curtain rises on Therese's house and Daniel's framework. Daniel is perched unmoving on the framework platform. Therese is standing at the kitchen table. Stage is completely dark except for a narrow blue spotlight falling on Therese, illuminating her from the waist up. She is utterly still and looking down.

A second blue spotlight illuminates the Television. This second light alternates between the Television and the Radio, depending on which voice is speaking.

Television
As we prepare to enter the twenty-first century, it is inevitable that it may be our last.

Therese
Another day, another nightmare.

Radio
The leading causes of death of men twenty-five to forty-four are heart disease, accident, homicide and AIDS. The leading causes of death for women twenty-five to forty-four are cancer, homicide, suicide and AIDS.

Therese
Getting out of bed is such a risk.

Television
Forty-seven percent of our population is barely literate, hundreds of thousands are unemployed. The majority of the homeless in our country are minors and despite efforts, drugs continue to claim thousands of lives each year.
Still, we only wonder if our military budget is too high.

Therese
Sweet priorities....

Radio
When one thousand four hundred-forty acres of rain forest are destroyed each day, and entire species of animals are threatened by man-made extinction, it is not surprising that the far-right has made hate a family value and outlawed diversity.

Therese
I think we lost our priorities with our decency. Or was it our humanity?

Television and Radio
We live so blindly the world would be a better place without us.

Therese
Why not be blind? Nothing to see but darkness anyway. Blind's not half bad.

Therese lifts the knife in both hands and thrusts down. General lights rise on Therese' house. (The framework remains in darkness.) Therese stands before a table. The knife is buried in an apple sitting on a cutting block. She cuts the apple into slices as she speaks.

Therese
But I search for meaning in the madness. What am I finding? Not meaning. Just more madness.
Mama, you always told me the story of the angel inside apples. You said, when you cut it just right, you can see her. The tiny body and the wings on either side. Everyone else says it's a star, but I believed you. It does look like an angel. A beautiful little angel. But you never told me that you have to sever the

seeds to see her. Sacrifice for beauty, huh, Mama? Sacrifice for perfection?

Therese slowly cuts the apple into smaller pieces.

<u>Therese</u>
That's the way the whole world is. You always have to give something up to gain something better. Taught to keep wanting, to do whatever it takes to want something else. A never-ending shopping experience. The risks we take to be ourselves. The risks we take knowing we can't change the world... can we?
It's such a waste. Why take the chance? Why be a light, when light reveals more horror?
Why be yourself, when you're killed for it?

<u>Television</u>
The average inner city child has seen someone shot before he is ten years old.

<u>Therese</u>
Darkness is a broken promise, uncomfortable silence... bad milk. Darkness leaves space for nothing. Where is innocence? Where is laughter? Where is there room for imagination?

Light illuminates Daniel's framework. (Therese's house stays lit.) Daniel stands on the topmost platform, her hands on her hips. She wears a tool belt furnished with a variety of tools, including two nail-guns. She is exuberant, playful, jumping from platform to platform, using a western accent.

<u>Daniel</u>
"Wrong, Bad Bart! Yer wrong!" Daniel High-Noon O'Donald swaggers out into Main Street. Oh, she's been awaitin'

this here day all her life. When the whole town would gather to see her face off with the crookedest cowboy either side of the Mason Dixon line!

"What's that, Bad Bart? You say only men can be cowboys? Oh, honey, don't go there."

High-Noon O'Donald tips back her hat with the lavender snake-skin band, her tool belt swung low on her hips as her twin Makita nail-guns glisten in the golden sun. She gives Bad Bart Bailey a sneer. "Didn' your mama ever teach you never to argue with a woman?"

Daniel pulls her nail-guns and shoots.

Daniel
Blam, blam, blam!

Daniel blows the smoke off each gun.

Daniel
Nail'd him!

Lights stay on the framework. Daniel moves through the actions of work. Therese, still dicing the apple with the knife, continues.

Therese
You search and you find shadows again and again, even when you're looking for light. Shadows... the pain of living, the fears. Then one day, the shadows become absolute. They become darkness with no end , no boundaries, no edge. But still you search. You search for something bright, vivid, brilliant, something totally alive. The light in the dark.

You're just walking down the street minding your own business and suddenly you realize that every day someone is shot just walking down the street minding their own business.

You decide to stay home.

We're born alone, we live alone and we die alone. Something to be said for consistency.

Radio

Every hour of every day children are battered. Most are abused by someone they know and trust: a parent, grandparent or sibling. By family.

Therese

What has searching found me? More questions to be answered. Can we really know anyone? What does trust mean? Risk? If trust is risk, then how much trust am I willing to give? How much trust can I put in my country? My government? Myself? How much am I willing to risk?

And who cares? No matter who you trust, no matter what you risk, every life ends the same. No matter how bitter or how sweet the journey.

Risk and mortality even sound like they go together, like two poisonous plants. "Don't touch the Risk, children. Don't play too close to the Mortality."

But mortality is the one thing that has no risk at all. There's no doubt. Someday, everyone dies.

Therese lays the knife aside, looking at the apple in shock. The apple is diced into bits. She picks up a handful.

Therese
Look, little bits of angels.

Therese walks to the counter. She gets two mugs and pours coffee in each. She brings the mugs back to the table but then only stands looking down at them. She looks over at her typewriter.

Therese

Mama... if you were here now, you could drink coffee with me. We could talk. You could listen to me... for the first time. With your two lumps of sugar I'd slip you a question and maybe with your first sip you'd drip an answer.

More than anything else in my life you baffled me. Told me a writer should write the truth. Write to bring light to the world. There's a contradiction right there. But you lived the greatest contradiction. You lived a lie and hid in the darkness whenever you could.

I lived in my words. My poems. Each was a micro world. What happened to them? They were washed away. A tidal wave came and washed them all away. A tidal wave with your name all over it, Mama. Because I'll never get any answers from you, will I? I'll die before you give me anything.

I'll just wait here, wanting, wondering, in this world without kindness, without answers. Where reaching out to someone just isn't in style anymore.

Daniel looks over her shoulder and stops work with a smile as she sees someone.

Daniel

Hey, Mrs. Blake! I was beginning to worry. Haven't seen ya around. Yeah, I guessed while Mr. Blake was on business you'd stay with your ma.

You're absolutely huge, girl! You look great! What are you now, seven months along? Eight?! Geez! And I thought unloading fifty pound bags of concrete was bad. At least I get to put them down – or tell George over here to carry 'em for me!

Well, hey! Don't you worry about anything with the addition here, okay? Even with the delay 'cause of those rainy weeks, you're still gonna have one gorgeous nursery when we're done! We'll even paint the walls with a construction motif: pink tools for a girl, blue tools for a boy! Or maybe purple tools for both?

And you tell Mr. Blake he better stay around home now. Remind him it took two to tango! He'd better finish the dance! See ya!

Daniel looks below, addresses her fellow worker.

Daniel

Georgie! Man, sometimes I think you were born with a hardhat instead of a brain. Would you tuck the back of your shirt in, or pull your pants up more, or something. I don't do crack, ya know? George Michael you ain't!

Don't give me no lip. Rule number one: the boss is always right. Rule number two: if she's not right, refer to rule number one – Hey!

Daniel waves a screwdriver at him.

Daniel
Screw you, George.

Daniel talks a bit more with George in mime and then goes back to work. Therese walks from the kitchen table to the desk. She stares down at the typewriter.

Therese

Mama, Mama.... I always wanted so many answers from you, always wanted to ask you so much. But I could never make you hear me. And now, you're dead. Now, you've drunk yourself away. And I think all your whiskey has just washed over my world, killing everything. You're gone and I'm afraid my whole life will be as incomplete as we are.

Life is a beautiful thing. The greatest gift. But not if we have to die without our answers! Everyone has questions. Things you just have to know. Why did he die? Why did she have to leave me? What's the difference between Bob Dole and Dole Pineapple? Without answers each day of living only brings me a day closer to the end. The... end.

Therese sits down at her desk.

Therese
Unless we deny it. Deny death. Make it wrong, ignore it, push it aside, insist that it doesn't exist. It's been done for hundreds of years with anything that society couldn't control. Anything with power. Anything we're afraid of. If society has taught me anything, it's how to invalidate what I don't believe. What doesn't share its power with me.

Deny death. I know life would be better if we did. Life would be longer. We'd save ourselves all those moments of fearing death or wondering where we go. We'd have more time to search for answers. Deny death. Maybe we should pass an initiative?

Television
Denial: rejection of a request or a rejection of the validity of a statement or a reality. Denial is one of the two components present in almost all destructive behaviors. The second component is fear.

Therese types on the manual typewriter at her desk.

Therese
In this world I'm finding... stone. Walls, monuments, cellars. Stones that mark boundaries, that show danger. How can it be that foundations are made of stone to keep us strong, but that stones are thrown away when we garden? Why do we say it's a virtue to have a will of stone, but that it's wrong to cast stones? Even our names are etched in stone, so that we'll never

be forgotten but only after we die. We have to die to become immortal.

Right now the world is all darkness and stone. Every time I think I see a little light, some other crisis strikes. Every time I think I find softness, some other trauma descends.

If I couldn't get any answers out of you, Mama, how will I ever get answers out of life? Call the Life Hotline? Hello Life Hotline, I was just wondering... is there anything stronger than death?!

I listen to all the reports. I read all the papers. There's no passion, no joy, no light or kindness left. There's no hope, no community. No humor!

Daniel jumps up onto a high crossbeam and drops backwards, swinging upside-down by her knees.

<u>Daniel</u>
There once was a girl from Norway,
who hung by her heels from a doorway.
So when you came in,
you would always grin,
as you buried your face in her—

A car honks twice. Daniel flips over onto her feet and tries to wave the car down.

<u>Daniel</u>
Ah, geez! Hey, Mrs. Blake, wait a second! Wait! Yeah, just wave back at me. Great! Very intelligent. Damn!

Daniel looks below at George.

<u>Daniel</u>
I just have to make this phone call, that's all. I was hoping I could use their phone.

Daniel jumps down off the framework. She strides a ways, hands on hips, looks over at Therese who is typing and ripping out sheets of paper, crumbling them and throwing them aside. Daniel walks back to the framework.

Daniel
Well, Ms. Tree Killer is at it again. How many sheets of paper did she go through that one day, Georgie? Like a hundred? Well, at least she won't be on the phone. If she has a phone!

Daniel starts walking away.

Daniel
So this gal calls up her friend and says, "You never go out. You never spend any time with me. What's wrong with you? You got some kind of social disease?" And her friend says, "Yeah, I'm a writer!"

Daniel laughs, walks off stage. Therese is typing with forced concentration. Blue lights flash between the Television and the Radio.

Therese
I was searching but was washed over with death. I cannot find the end to the dark, so there is no light to show me my answers. I cannot find what is stronger than death, because I can search no more, only fumble into more shadows. If I can't have answers, then I can't have questions. But I do. So I won't have a deadline instead. Death cannot exist.

Radio
Three point nine million Americans work for minimum wage or less. Sixty-five percent of these are women. Most of these women have families – children who grow up not knowing

what hunger means because they've known nothing else.

Television

Sex crime. Even after raping a woman because her dress was too tight, a rapist can walk the streets again. Because the victim asked for it. And so did the next woman.

Therese

Darkness cannot reach me. Death cannot reach me.

Radio

A man can brutally slaughter his wife and children, then receive life imprisonment and be supported by our tax dollars. Yet hundreds of students will never receive the scholarships they need to fund a college education, and twelve million adults and millions of children will go hungry each day.

Television

Hate crime. Even after beating a man to death because his walk was too feminine, a killer can walk the street again. Because the victim asked for it. And so did the next man.

Therese

If death knocks, I will not answer.

A knock sounds. Stage lights cut. Therese is struck with a red spotlight. The knock comes again.

Therese

I don't hear anything.... I don't hear–

Daniel steps out of the darkness in front of Therese, peering in a window from outside. Therese screams. When she stops, Daniel speaks loud enough to be heard through the window as the red spotlight is replaced by stage lights.

Daniel
Can I use your phone?

Therese
Death wants to use my phone?

Daniel
What? I can't hear you through the window. Can you hear me? I want to use your phone, to make a call? Ya know, call someone? I'm from the construction site across the street, and the client left before I could use theirs.

Therese leans forward and opens the window.

Therese
Using the phone would be fine.

Daniel
Should I crawl in the window?

Therese
No, come to the door. It's faster.

Therese stands and walks to the door. Daniel follows.

Daniel
Do not climb in the window. Do not adjust your mental stability. You are entering the Tree Killer Zone.

Therese unlocks the door. Daniel walks in, boldly looking around. Therese closes the door behind her and leans against the frame. She watches Daniel. Daniel points to the crumpled papers.

Daniel
Hope you recycle... all those dead trees, ya know.

Therese looks blankly at the papers, then extends a hand.
Daniel backs away sharply, avoiding all contact. They both look
at Therese's hand and then meet eyes. Therese drops her hand.

Therese
The paper's hemp, and I'm Therese Weaver.

Daniel
The poet.

Therese
You know me?

Daniel
No.

They stare at each other in silence.

Daniel
A friend of mine has some of your books.

Therese
Oh.

They stare at each other in silence.

Daniel
Phone?

Therese takes the phone from inside a drawer in the
counter, removing a pile of papers and odd-and-ends first. She
hands it to Daniel who plucks it from her hand.

Daniel
Don't use it much, huh?

Daniel chuckles and goes to dial, but stops because Therese is standing next her. Daniel steps away. Therese continues to watch her. Daniel looks back at her over her shoulder and finally points down at the two coffee mugs.

Daniel
Your coffees are getting cold.

Therese takes the coffee mugs. Daniel dials. Therese puts one cup on the counter, the other in the microwave.

Daniel
Yes, I'll hold.

Daniel looks at Therese who is standing in front of the microwave.

Daniel
Don't stand too close to that. The radiation will kill ya.

Daniel turns and mimes speaking on the phone. When Daniel's back is turned, Therese jumps away from the microwave and yanks the plug out, eyeing the machine in open terror. Daniel's voice rises with increasing aggravation. Therese watches Daniel.

Daniel
Yeah, I know I scheduled it for today. But I do work for a living. No, I can't imagine many things more important than keeping a roof over my head and food in my mouth! Yeah, well, HMO to you too.

Daniel reaches out and absently picks up a handful of diced apple. She chews, making grunting noises at the receiver, and then makes a face, looking down at the pile of fruit. She picks up a single piece to show Therese.

Daniel
Hey look, an angel.

Daniel turns back to phone.

Daniel
This will be the first time I see him, actually. Just tell him, we can meet next month... or the month after that would be fine. Well, I prefer one day at a time, but thanks for your support.
No, I don't want to talk with him. Fine! If he steps in, in the next sixty seconds, have him call me at home.

Daniel looks down at the phone, reading Therese's number.

Daniel
It's 937-5524. But if he doesn't reach me, I'll just call next year! Yeah, have a day yourself, Nurse Ratchet.

Daniel hangs up.

Daniel
Not a School of Personality graduate! Cult of Personality perhaps....

Daniel looks over at Therese. Still holding the phone, Daniel walks towards the door. Therese walks slowly to the table and stands staring at the apple bits. Therese picks up the piece that Daniel found.

Daniel
Thanks for letting me use your phone, Therese.

Therese
You really did find the angel.

Daniel smiles playfully for a moment, moving closer to Therese.

Daniel
Yeah. The wings still have the seeds in 'em – they're not even cut in half!

Therese looks at Daniel. Daniel realizes suddenly how close they are standing and backs away abruptly.

Therese
You didn't tell me your name.

Daniel
Daniel O'Donald of O'Donald Construction. "If we can't build it, you don't need it!"

The phone rings. They both jump. Daniel answers it.

Daniel
Hello? Oh sorry, you just missed Ms. O'Donald. Yeah? Well, life's tough sometimes. Bye.

Daniel puts the phone down on the table, looking pleased.

Daniel
It was for me.

Daniel looks at Therese. Therese is staring intently at the apple piece. Daniel watches her a bit and then goes to touch her shoulder, but at the last minute Daniel turns and takes hold of the door knob instead.

Daniel

Hey, Therese?

Therese looks over at her. Daniel turns and faces her, keeping her hand on the door.

Daniel

You know, I don't mean to pry, but I have this crazy problem – I care about people... strange people. I've kinda noticed that you sit and type a lot, you almost couldn't find your phone and there's apple shit all over your table... maybe you should get out more.

Daniel raises a finger to make a point.

Daniel

A friend gave me some advice once. She said, "Get a life." It completely changed me!

Therese cracks a smile.

Therese

I'll keep that in mind.

Daniel opens the door to go. Therese is still holding onto the apple angel.

Therese

Is it really Daniel? Like Daniel in the lion's den?

Daniel pauses with a solemn grin.

Daniel
Yeah. It's just like that.

Daniel walks off stage. Therese looks from the closed door to the apple angel. Her hand holding the angel creeps to her heart as she speaks.

Therese
I ask again... what is the one thing that death doesn't end? What lives even when you die?

So Daniel, you care? "Get a life." Does it come with a side of answers?

The phone rings. Therese looks at it for a minute. Then she picks it up with one hand, keeping the angel in the other hand.

Therese
Yes? No, I'm sorry she just.... She was here before, but now.... No, I'm not.... But I'm not....

....You're absolutely right, Doctor. You're absolutely right.

Slowly Therese lowers the angel, dropping it onto the table. Stage lights slowly go out, leaving Therese in a white spotlight. Blue spotlights strike both the Radio and the Television when they speak and then stay lit.

Radio
In the time it takes to say these words, a woman will be raped.

Therese
No, Doctor, I shouldn't joke around like I did, pretending I wasn't me... Daniel.
Yes, this is very serious. Joking is irresponsible.
Yes, skipping appointments is irresponsible too. I'll try to think things through a little more. Please apologize to Nurse Kelly. Oh? All right. I suppose Monday will be fine. I look forward to working with you too. Thank you, Doctor. Have a good day.

Therese hangs up the phone.

Television
People are practicing safer sex because of the rising threat of sexually transmitted disease. No one wants to be dying of AIDS.

Therese
What about living with it?

Curtain falls. Act One ends.

Act Two
At the Edge

Scene One

Curtain remains down. Framework lighted. On the platform, there is a can of nails. Across the stage from the framework and in darkness, hangs a sign over the cafe setting. There is a table with two chairs and a standing plant. Daniel stands on the smaller platform of the framework, wearing work gloves and tool belt. She is arguing with George below.

<u>Daniel</u>
So before the election, we're promised a national health plan. We're promised anti-discrimination laws and equal opportunities, the right to fight for our country. Good promises. And very shrewd promises too!

Gays and lesbians are loud voters. We need that health plan, because our Brothers – and our Sisters! – are dying. And we need laws that make sure we're treated like everyone else. That make sure if we come Out, we won't lose our jobs – or our lives!

But let me tell ya... if we don't get the rights, than I ain't fighting for this country. Military ban or no military ban! They let us die without insurance. They let us be beaten on the streets – I'm not giving them another way to kill me!

What'd you say?

Just give 'em a chance, huh? Change takes time?

Daniel squats down and glares.

<u>Daniel</u>
Some of us don't have time!

Daniel jumps to the lower platform and starts hammering loudly. Her back is turned when Therese steps up. Therese pauses, looking at Daniel. Therese jumps like someone

*has tapped her shoulder, spins around, then relaxes as she sees
George. She mimes speaking with George as Daniel's
hammering continues. Therese points to Daniel, then mimes
shaking hands with George. Therese walks over below Daniel
and calls up to her. Daniel is hammering and doesn't hear,
Therese calls again.*

<u>Therese</u>
Daniel O'Donald!

<u>Daniel</u>
What?!

Daniel sees Therese and stops her work.

<u>Daniel</u>
Hey! The poet!

<u>Therese</u>
I wanted to stop by and apologize for yesterday. I haven't
had visitors for while, and you... you caught me by surprise. I'm
sorry I acted so strangely.

<u>Daniel</u>
Aah, I never should have scared you like that. Besides, I
always figured poets were strange.

<u>Therese</u>
Well, you were right... about me not having been out in a
while. Your advice was heard. You got me thinking.

Daniel laughs, not quite knowing what to make of this.

<u>Daniel</u>
Huh. Yeah, 'bout getting a life? That's part of my

personal philosophy. Just think – all that wisdom and tying up your phone to boot!

Therese
What's the other part? Of your personal philosophy.

Daniel
I call it the Four Step Program. Get a life. Keep a life. Snap out of it. Stay out of it. What do ya think? Should I put it on a tee-shirt?

Therese
I'd buy one.

Daniel
My fortune's made. I just have this habit of getting into other people's business.

Therese
A habit of caring?

Daniel
Just getting my two cents in.

Therese
Caring.

Therese pauses.

Therese
I also wanted to give you this.

Therese hands Daniel a piece of paper. Daniel keeps her gloves on; their hands do not touch. Once Daniel has the paper, she takes off her gloves, keeping them in one hand. Daniel speaks with rising anger.

Daniel
You couldn't just tell me my doctor called... that you'd made an appointment for me? You had to write it down?

Therese
Well... it was actually your doctor who made the appointment. He didn't believe that I wasn't you. Apparently, you've pulled stunts like that before, and he heard about them from your old physician. And I wrote everything down to bring to you, because I knew there was another worker, and I didn't know, if we would be able to... speak freely–

Daniel
George and I are in the same support group.

Therese looks over at George.

Therese
Oh.

Daniel
Yeah, oh.

Therese
You really should go in more often.

Daniel
In?

Therese
For... check ups.

Daniel speaks with frustration and anger.

> **Daniel**
> Check up? What's to check? I'm dying! Where do you get off–

> **Therese**
> Why don't you want help? Why don't you–

> **Daniel**
> Who the hell do you think you–

> **Therese**
> The doctors might be able to–

Daniel jumps down in front of Therese.

> **Daniel**
> Listen to me, Therese Weaver! I live my life the way I please and call it what I like. I have my own rules! My own way! I accept that it's my fault you got involved in this. But let's get something straight – when I told you to get a life, I meant one of your own!

They stand in silence. Daniel's anger does not intimidate Therese. Therese speaks first, quietly.

> **Therese**
> You're so alive....

> **Daniel**
> What?!

> **Therese**
> Bravery. Light.... How do you do it?

Daniel
You're a lunatic. Therese! Snap out f it! What are you
talking about?

                        Therese
I just feel like I want to talk to you. Ask you questions.

                        Daniel
            Okay. So ask me. I'll answer you.

                        Therese
                  You'll answer....

                        Daniel
                  Hello? Therese?

                        Therese
            You should go see your doctor.

                        Daniel
                That wasn't a question.

                        Therese
            You'd feel better about yourself.

                        Daniel
                Thank you, Jiminey.

                  Daniel turns away.

                        Therese
Daniel, I'm going to have dinner at The Edge Cafe.
Would you...?

> ### Daniel
> You're asking me out?!

> ### Therese
> No! Well... just if you happened to be there, feel free to join me.

Daniel backs away abruptly to let Therese pass. Therese pauses to say good-bye to George.

> ### Therese
> It was a pleasure to meet you, George.

Therese mimes shaking George's hand. She shoots Daniel a glare.

> ### Therese
> At least someone still has the courtesy to shake hands.

Therese walks off stage. Daniel stares after her, then throws her gloves down.

> ### Daniel
> I should have used a payphone.

Lights go down. Scene One ends.

Scene Two

*Spotlight comes up on Therese as she stands to the side
of the stage. On the opposite side of the stage is the cafe sign
and the table; there are silverware and napkins laid out. A large
potted plant stands by the table.*
Therese slowly moves across the stage. Spotlight follows.
She is hesitant.

<u>Therese</u>
So I begin again. Out into the world.

A blue light spots Therese with a voice.

<u>Panhandler</u>
Hey, lady? Can you spare some change? I haven't eaten–

<u>Therese</u>
I'm sorry. I – oh, well... here.

*Therese turns away. A green light spots her with another
voice.*

<u>Prostitute</u>
Hey, Darlin'.... You'd be amazed what fifty dollars can
buy–

<u>Therese</u>
No! No, thank you. I–

*Therese steps away. A red light spots her with another
voice.*

<u>Pusher</u>
You're awful jumpy, sweet-thing. I could take care of

that real easy, though. These little beauties–

Therese hurries away. A light spots the cafe sign and Daniel who stands under it. Therese comes to a stop.

Daniel
You did say The Edge, right?

Therese
I certainly did.

Daniel
Well, glad to see you stopped by.

Daniel mimes opening the cafe door and walks in, leaving Therese outside. Therese relaxes. Daniel opens the door again.

Daniel
Any time now. I'd rather not die of starvation.

Daniel lets go of the door, turns to look around the cafe.

Therese
So much for chivalry!

Therese enters the cafe to join her. The sounds of the cafe rise, people talking and eating. They both look around. Daniel adopts a snobbish accent.

Daniel
Well! We've never had a poet grace us before. Where do you care to sit, Ms. Weaver?

Therese
The covered porch is nice—

Therese reaches to touch Daniel's arm as she points to the table. Daniel dodges Therese's hand, moves to the table and seats herself. She is reading her menu when Therese joins her.

Daniel
We might want to move the table back some. We'll get a lot of street noise out here.

Therese
Just pick the table up and move it? I'm sure we'll be fine if we stay—

Car horns and traffic sounds drown her out. Therese looks towards the street. Daniel puts her menu down, yelling above the noise.

Daniel
You're sure of what?

Therese frowns. They move the table and chairs towards center stage. Therese sits and picks up her menu. Daniel remains standing. Daniel looks from the tall potted plant to Therese and back again. Therese looks up.

Therese
What?
Oh God, Daniel. Please no!

Daniel
It looks so lonely....

<u>Therese</u>

It looks fine! Daniel, there are four other couples out here. Please don't embarrass–

<u>Daniel</u>

Haven't quiet got a life yet, have ya?

Daniel goes to the plant. Therese watches. Daniel greets the plant with exaggerated delight, then embraces it.

<u>Daniel</u>

Flora?! Is that you, sweetheart? Well, oh my good Goddess, I never would have recognized you! You know I haven't seen you in – why! It's been seasons!

Are you using fertilizer, gal? No? Then you must be wearing your leaves different? You look marvelous.

Daniel turns to include the patrons around her as well as Therese.

<u>Daniel</u>

Doesn't she look great? You know, she does! Well, Flora sweetheart, why don't you join us? Hmm? Maybe some water? My goodness, you're parched.

Daniel picks up the plant with a grunt.

<u>Daniel</u>

You've put on some weight, Flora! But I always have liked my greenery lush.

Daniel sets the plant down next to their table and looks to the other patrons.

> Daniel

You know, if you move away from us like that, you'll be bothered by the noise from the street.

Traffic sounds rise.

> Daniel
> Told ya.

Daniel sits and picks up her menu. Therese watches her. Daniel looks up, uneasy.

> Daniel
> What are you doing?

> Therese
> Watching you.

> Daniel
> Why?

> Therese
> Because you make me laugh.

> Daniel
> I thought I embarrassed you?

> Therese
> It's good for me.

> Daniel
> You must be Republican.

Daniel looks back at her menu but Therese is still watching her and it makes her uncomfortable.

> Daniel
> Do you read the Sunday comics?

> Therese
> Yes.

> Daniel
> Do they make you laugh?

> Therese
> "Sylvia" makcs me laugh.

> Daniel
> Do you look at "Sylvia" like you look at me?

> Therese
> No.

> Daniel
> You shouldn't look at people like that.

> Therese
> Why?

> Daniel
> You shouldn't look at me like that!

> Therese
> Why?!

> Daniel
> People just don't! Especially people... who have talked to
my doctor.

Therese
Well, I'm not people.

Daniel
I'm having dinner with the creature from the black lagoon.

Therese
And I didn't talk to your doctor. You talked to your doctor.

Daniel
I knew poets were strange.

Therese
Daniel, thank you for coming.

Daniel
Hey... anytime you need someone to insult you, embarrass you, call you a creature, tell you to get a life – I'm there!

Therese
Insult me? Is that what you were doing? I thought you were being charming.

Daniel
You're twisted.

Therese
I'm certainly not straight.

Daniel
I just came to see if you were going to apologize.

Therese
For what?

Daniel
For intruding on my life and making me an appointment
with my doctor.

Therese
Like you intruded on my life and got me out of the
house? Sounds like we both needed some intrusion.

Daniel
Does that mean I don't get an apology?

Therese
Not on your life.

Daniel
What's left of it!

Therese is taken aback by Daniel's humor.

Therese
I'm – I'm not apologizing.

Daniel
Good. I can't stand a woman without a back bone.
Except for Flora here.

A leaf drops from the plant.

Daniel
Is it autumn already?

Therese
Waiter! I think we're ready. One check will be fine.

Daniel puts a hand to her heart, adopting a southern accent.

Daniel
Are you offerin' to buy me dinner, Ms. Weaver?

Therese
I certainly am, Ms. O'Donald. If you don't object?

Daniel
By golly, that's so sweet of you.

Daniel stands quickly, spins her chair around and sits again, straddling the chair. She drops the southern accent.

Daniel
Yeah, like I really need someone to buy my meals. I'm sure you poets make much more than us construction company owners.

Therese
Fine.
Could we make this separate checks? Thank you.
Better?

Daniel
Much.

Therese
I'll have your halibut, please. And how about a bottle of your house white wine.

Daniel
A whole bottle? That's being a bit excessive, isn't it? I don't wanna have to carry you home!

Therese
Since you won't even shake my hand, I don't think carrying me home will become an issue. Anyway, it never tastes right by the glass. And there are two of us.

Daniel
Ahh, but I don't drink. And white wine wouldn't go well with my hamburger, even if I did.

Therese
All right. Forget the wine. I'll have an espresso.

Daniel
You drink concentrated caffeine, alcohol, and you stand in front of microwaves. Wanna bet on which one of us lives longer?

Therese
Fine! Water? Can I have some water?!

Daniel
I don't know. Can you?

Therese
I'll have a glass of ice water, please.

Daniel
Hope it's pure.

Therese laughs and addresses their waiter again.

Therese
Is the water here pure? Very pure? Great. We'll have two glasses of water, please.

Daniel
Can you believe that? She's ordering for me? I'll have a non-dairy shake, hold the fruit juice, and a hamburger with nothing on it minus the meat and the top bun.

Therese
What?

Daniel
Oh – please.

Therese
Daniel! You just ordered a cup of crushed ice and a bottom bun.

Daniel
I said please.

Therese
Just bring her a shake and a burger. Thanks.

Daniel
Well, if they don't do special orders...?

Therese
You need special help! Like one of those white jackets that ties in the back!

Daniel
I never could find shoes to match those.

<u>Therese</u>
I bet you've never matched shoes to anything in your life.
I was surprised you didn't show up in your tool belt.

<u>Daniel</u>
Well, usually I just take the tools out and put my
silverware in. But I thought, why not be different for a change?
Take a risk!

<u>Therese</u>
And they do have such nice silverware here.

<u>Daniel</u>
Very nice.

<u>Therese</u>
Nice company too.

<u>Daniel</u>
I didn't see company on the menu. Was that with the side
orders?

<u>Therese</u>
Could've sworn it was there. Right next to the meatless
burgers with no top bun.

<u>Daniel</u>
Must've missed it.

*They sit in silence. Daniel starts to whistle. Therese turns
to the plant.*

<u>Therese</u>
Flora, huh? It has a nice ring to it.

Daniel
It means plant. It's like calling a cat, Cat.

Therese covers the plant's ears.

Therese
You'll hurt her feelings!

Daniel
Very protective. You should have been a mother.

Therese
No, I don't like kids. Never have.

Daniel
Course not. Not a butch dyke like you.

Therese
Not a... like me...? Oh, no. It's just that I never got along
– you know, when I was a kid – with other kids.

Daniel
Loner?

Therese
Writer.

Daniel
Writer?

Therese
I was really close to my father. He died when I was six
and I became very serious about life.

Daniel
At six?

Therese
Yeah. Daddy died of lung cancer. Never smoked a cigarette in his life. I had a long time to be face to face with death... to think about things. At some point, someone explained to me that when you're done with your "life's reason," then you die. So I started wondering, stared searching... and I was always writing down what I found.

Daniel
Searching for this "reason?"

Therese
Searching for whatever it is that makes us wanna live. Why are we here? Why do we bother?

It seems that we're dead before we're born and we're dead after we die. So it has to be something pretty grand that makes us want to live, if the majority of our time is spent dead!

Daniel
You lost me.

Therese
I was searching for something stronger than death.

Daniel
Did you find it?

Therese
It hasn't been as easy as I thought it would be. Looking so closely at life show you things you might not want to know. But I'm still looking. What is it that survives death? That death doesn't end? What makes us want to live so badly that we stay

and fight and–

> Daniel
> Love.

Long pause.

> Therese
> Love?

> Daniel
> Yeah, love. Who was your first love? You know... who was the woman who saw through all that searching and scribbling and found a human being?

> Therese
> Oh....

> Daniel
> Aw Therese! Hey, I said "woman" because your poetry books are published by a feminist press. And you joked, so I just assumed. I mean, I guess I can still be your friend, if you're straight–?

Therese laughs.

> Therese
> No, it's not that. I am a...

> Daniel
> Lesbian?

Therese nods.

Therese
My first love would have to be my junior high gym teacher.
Daniel laughs.

Therese
Well, not my real first love. But she was the first person who saw someone other than the quiet, little kid. It was the day I got tangled between my jump rope and the volleyball net.

Daniel laughs again. Therese throws a napkin at her.

Therese
Now my first real love was when I was nineteen. I started college and met Tessie.

Daniel
Tell me you called her Tess?

Therese
No, Tessie.

Daniel
Oohhh.

Therese
Don't make me throw this fork at you.

Daniel
Fine name, Tessie. Fine name. Wish I had it myself.

Therese
We met in creative writing class.

Daniel
You found yourself with another writer? Thank the

Goddess, you couldn't breed.

Therese waves the fork.

<u>Therese</u>
So, we used to get together after class and read poetry to each other–

<u>Daniel</u>
Let me guess. Sappho and Emily Dickenson?

<u>Therese</u>
And Adreinne Rich.

<u>Daniel</u>
Oo, a live one.

Therese threatens with the fork again. Daniel picks up her own fork and mimes stabbing her own shoulder.

<u>Therese</u>
Enough–!

<u>Daniel</u>
So?

<u>Therese</u>
We were together for three years, and then she decided to spend her senior year abroad. Every week we wrote, exchanging poems... and promises. Then about a month before she was due home, her letters stopped coming.

<u>Daniel</u>
Found herself an overseas' gal, huh?

Therese
No... she was killed in a car accident.

Daniel
My God....

Therese
We'd never told anyone about us, and no one found where Tessie had been keeping my letters. I read about the accident in the university paper.

Daniel
Does everyone in your life die, Therese?

Therese
Everyone dies, Daniel.

Daniel
And that doesn't scare you? Death doesn't scare you?

Therese
Death is unknown. So yes, it's terrifying. But the more fearful it is, then the more beautiful the reason for living must be.

Sometimes, the world and all the darkness in it... sometimes that scares me. But on the whole, life is much scarier than death. The thing that really terrifies me is dying before I find my answers.

Daniel
So you're still searching.

Therese
Still searching.
There's our waiter – poor guy.

Therese rises and moves off stage. She returns quickly with dinner plates and glasses. Daniel watches as Therese sets things down and returns to her seat.

Therese
They're just so busy today....

Daniel
Pretty good balance. Were you a waitress?

Therese
No, just an avid reader. Balancing all those piles of books.

A toast, to my first dinner with Daniel at The Edge. With luck, it's far from the last.

Daniel
With luck.
Hmm... pure.

Therese
Very pure.

They laugh.

Therese
So tell me about your loves. First love and first real love.

Daniel
First love would have to be Vicki. I was eighteen. She was thirty. One night I was sitting at a bus stop. Vicki drove up in a brand new pick-up truck and asked if I needed a ride to heaven.

Therese
No wonder you thought my gym teacher story was tame!

Daniel
Kitten-tame. So, I told her she could keep dreamin', 'cause I wasn't that easy. She drove around the block, and when she stopped the second time, she threw me a hundred dollar bill.

Well, she didn't have to dream anymore. My parents had thrown me out of the house three weeks before and a hundred dollars was just about how easy I was. Hell, I was probably ten dollars easy!

Therese
I think I'll stick with jump ropes and volleyball nets.

Daniel
Yeah. Ms. Tangled-Up-So-Teacher-Can-Save-Me.

Therese
What about your first real love? Or is that an even worse story?

Daniel
She was a politician.

Therese
That is worse.

Daniel
Actually, she just worked with politicians. She was a lobbyist. Must admit, she's the one who got me up and active in the community.

Ha! Friends said, she imbued me with militancy.

Therese
So you're a carpenter and an activist, uh?

Daniel
Indeed. Street corners, soap boxes, conferences. Anywhere they'll have me. Anywhere I can sneak in.

Therese
What did she look like?

Daniel
Dark, handsome. Eyes that would stop you in your tracks. The kind of eyes you don't ever forget. Five two, hundred sixty-five pounds. Lots of fire. Sharp. A little wild, a little more mysterious.

Therese
Sounds like you really loved her. Like you made a good match.

Daniel
Well, I thought so. The day I tested positive, she packed her bags and moved out. Left behind the ring I bought her, nothing else. Didn't even ask how.

Therese reaches for Daniel's hand, then stops. Therese places her hand beside Daniel's on the table top.

Therese
Everyone says that our community embraces diversity. That we have pride in each other. Sometimes I don't know. You'd think there'd be more support. I mean, we know what it's like to be treated badly, to be cast aside from society's mainstream because we're... different. But no one even talks about... women... with–

Daniel

You won't say the word "lesbian."

Therese

Pardon?

Daniel

Lesbian. That's the third time you've worked yourself around saying that you're a lesbian.

Therese looks around at the other patrons.

Therese

Daniel, please.

Daniel

Therese Weaver! You write for a feminist press and you aren't Out?

Therese

I'm Out. I'm very proud of who I am.

Therese indicates the other patrons.

Therese

I just don't want to offend anyone.

Daniel

Therese, these are the nineties. The Stonewall Riot has already happened. Gays and lesbians are on the covers of magazines. We're fighting for our rights, showing the world that we exist and can no longer be ignored. If you don't want to hide, there's no reason! Take a stand!

Therese

It's different for you. You... build things, and wear your hair short, have that devil-may-care attitude. I look like... a poet. I'd have to do something drastic–

Daniel

I've known some wild poets, Therese. And I don't think people assume we're sisters or college buddies here. They know, sweetheart. They know.

Therese is skeptical. Daniel stands and looks at the patrons.

Therese
Daniel, what are you doing?

Daniel

I'm waiting for couple number five to be seated. Life is too short to shit around, Therese.

Sounds of customers rise.

Daniel

Ladies and gentlemen, if I may have your attention for just a moment please.

Chatter dies.

Daniel

Thank you. My name is Daniel O'Donald, and I have dedicated my life to helping those unfortunate lesbians who feel forced into the perpetual closet by often well-meaning but ignorant, straight folks.

Therese
Daniel....

Daniel
Now looking around me today, I can see that you are all far from ignorant but rather a more progressive – dare I say? – a more superior group of heterosexuals, who would never err so much as to pass judgment on another person simply because she may love those of her own gender?
No! I think instead, you would celebrate her happiness!
So then, reminding you that I try to help my lesbian Sisters who believe they will be stuck in the closet forever... I'd like to introduce my dear Sister, Therese Weaver.

Therese jumps up in shock.

Therese
Daniel!

Daniel cuts her off with a long kiss. Therese relaxes slowly. Then Therese's hand touches Daniel's, and Daniel wraps her arms about Therese. They draw away from each other slowly.

Daniel
Didn't she do great, folks?

Applause answer her and Daniel joins in. Therese looks around. When applause dies down, she points to Daniel.

Therese
She's always like this when she escapes from the convent.

Applause sounds again.

Therese
Thank you. Thank you....

Therese addresses Daniel.

Therese
What? We're national treasures now? Where's the applause sign?

They sit back down. Applause fades.

Therese
So is this really a hobby of yours? Creative Outing? I mean, do arts and crafts not do it for you?

Daniel
I build things with power tools, not glue sticks. What about you? Anything besides writing and crumpling up paper?

Therese
I play backgammon.

Daniel
You really haven't dated in a while. What kind of music do you listen to?

Therese
Oh, it varies. Meg, Cris, Holly....

Daniel
What?

Therese
Meg Christian, Cris Williamson, Holly Near.

Daniel
It's the 1970s revisited.
Melissa Ethridge, k.d. lang...?

Therese
Who?

Daniel
I thought you read the papers? What was the last lesbian film you saw?

Therese
Oh, Daniel. Like there's been more than one. "Desert Hearts," of course.

Daniel despairs.

Daniel
"Claire of the Moon" mean anything to you?

Therese
As in classical music?

Daniel
"Go Fish?"

Therese
The game?

Daniel
Last lesbian book you read? And don't say—

Therese and Daniel
"Rubyfruit Jungle."

Daniel

Nooooo....

"Curious Wine," "Bitter Thorns," "S/he," "Sparks Might Fly"... "Escape to the Wind?!" Lesbians have books in every genre now, ya know?

Therese

I did hear that Rita Mae Brown came out with another book. Non-fiction, I guess. Something about the solar system. "Venus Envy?"

Daniel

Last try, Therese. When I say "tennis," who do you think of?

Therese

I was never really into sports–

Daniel

Martina, Therese! You think of Martina Navratilova! Nine time Wimbledon winner and Out lesbian! Oh Therese!

Therese

I told you, I haven't been out in a while!

Daniel

A while? A while?! We've put a man on the moon, sweetheart.

Daniel starts searching around, under the table, under the napkin and so on.

Therese

What are you doing?

<u>Daniel</u>
Okay, where is it?

<u>Therese</u>
Where's what?

<u>Daniel</u>
The time warp you've been stuck in!

<u>Therese</u>
"Time warp!" "The Rocky Horror Picture Show!" There!
I do know one!

<u>Daniel</u>
Yeah, but one what?

Lights dim. Scene Two ends.

Scene Three

It's after dinner. Therese and Daniel have remained at the cafe, but they have moved to the side of the patio to enjoy an ocean view and the sunset. They sit on the stage, dangling their feet over the edge, drinking root beer. Daniel drinks hers from the bottle; Therese drinks hers from a glass. They sit in a pool of light. A second light shines on The Edge Cafe sign. Their table is pushed back to one side of the stage.

<u>Therese</u>
They say if gays and lesbians start raising children, getting legally married, it will ruin the moral fabric of the American family. Seems to me that heterosexuals have had their chance and look at kids today! It's time for us to take over.

<u>Daniel</u>
I used to feel that way about our country. I mean, men have always been president and look where it's gotten us. I'm glad we have a woman running things now.

<u>Therese</u>
It took me forever to realize that Hillary wasn't the Clinton everyone was talking about.

<u>Daniel</u>
That's because she was.

Daniel leans over the edge of the stage.

<u>Daniel</u>
This place really is the edge. Drops straight down to the ocean.
A second toast! To the moonlight, to Flora, to poets... and to beer, of the root variety!

Therese
Yes, to root beer without caffeine and without sugar!

Daniel
To useless, tasteless – but pure – brown water!

Therese and Daniel
Hmm!

Therese
And to carpenters. If they can't build it, you don't need it!
And we sat at The Edge,
on the edge 'bove the sea,
toasting the moonlight, us
...and thee!

Daniel
I hate poetry that rhymes. Only limericks should rhyme.

Therese
Limericks are poetry.

Daniel
I'm more cultured than I thought! Have you heard the
one:

There once was a girl from Norway,
who hung by her heels from the doorway.
So when you walked in,
you would always grin,
as you buried your face in her–

Therese
That won't rhyme.

Daniel
Yes it does!

Therese
If you say it with a drawl.

Daniel
Ex-act-lay!

Therese
That doesn't count.

Daniel
Oh, just suck the joy out of life for me! Go ahead! Just suck it right out. Leave my bones marrowless and hollow, brittle in the harsh winds to fall to dust and be blown away, blown, blown, blown....

Daniel collapses with a clonk of her head against the stage.

Therese
You okay, Ms. Melodrama?

Daniel
Well, I'm dying.

Pause. Therese continues seriously.

Therese
Your doctor, does he give you drugs... um, medicine... to help?

Daniel
Drugs. Yes. Sometimes I take them. Sometimes I don't.

Everything is experimental. No one knows what they're doing. Anyway, it's quality of life that's important, not quantity.

Therese

What do you think about the stuff you're taking...? Or alternative treatments... therapies?

Daniel

I think for some people anything can work a miracle. I think for me, it's all just hope. False hope. Why spend so much time on pipe dreams?

Therese
Dreams keep us alive.

Daniel
No, reality keeps you alive. Dreams you wake up from.

Long pause. Therese stares into her glass. Daniel fidgets, then stands.

Daniel

Okay, Therese! Enough of that. You have an overwhelmed look on your face. You're searching again!

I saw you reaching for pieces of paper to crumple. This could get dangerous. I'd like to try to do this more often – get you out of the house, I mean. But it won't do any good if you drift away, you know? OooOooOoo!

Daniel makes ghostly motions.

Therese
Sorry. I just slip beneath it all sometimes.

Daniel sits and pretends to take notes.

<u>Daniel</u>
And how long has this been happening, Ms. Weaver?

Therese plays along.

<u>Therese</u>
On and off since I was six. More on than off for the past couple months.

<u>Daniel</u>
My prescription: Let Daniel take you out three times a week.
Not for dates. Just little jaunts. Kind of like walking a dog.

<u>Therese</u>
I get to put you on a leash?

<u>Daniel</u>
I believe you have a serious case of role reversal. I'll be walking you, the resident poet. Great way to meet women.

Daniel adopts a snobbish accent.

<u>Daniel</u>
Oh my! Is that an eccentric native poet? How ever did you find one?

Therese matches Daniel's accent.

<u>Therese</u>
I simply must have four of them!

Daniel
So sorry, darling. This one doesn't breed.

Therese
Just ask anyone at The Edge last Friday night!

Daniel
So, is that a yes?

Therese
Um, walking here was... quite an experience. Maybe we could just stay at my place?

Daniel
That kinda negates you getting out of the house.

Therese
We could talk about things outside the house.

Daniel
Therese, though it reassures me that we wouldn't just talk about your microwave, I'd like to go somewhere where I can see something other than your wallpaper. I mean, I'm dying here, you know? I'd like to get the most out of my time!

Therese
Why do you do that?! Why do you constantly give it such power? Always bring it up?

Daniel
Wallpaper?

Therese
Death!

Daniel
Why do I say the word "lesbian?" Not just because I'm well adjusted. I take claim. I've accepted myself. And I want others to know what they're getting into. Death is part of who I am just as much as being a lesbian. Can you understand that?

Therese
I understand that you make me feel alive! More alive than I've ever felt. I want to spend time with you. Living time, for God's sake! Is that too much to ask?

Daniel
Yes! I can't love a woman who isn't willing to watch me die!

They both fall suddenly silent, realizing what their words imply.

Therese
Part of me would die with you.

Daniel
You'd hurt, but you wouldn't die. You'd live and living is a lot harder than dying.

Therese
I'd never leave you.

Daniel
I'd be doing the leaving.

Therese
You always have to be in control, don't you? Make all the choices?

Daniel
I didn't choose to die young. I do choose to live without

denial, no matter how bad things get.

People are afraid of what they don't know. If you only skirt something – only glimpse it – you'll always feel fear it. I've looked death in the face, in the eye, and accepted it. I'm dying. I can't change that.

I think you've looked at it too. You know death, but something has scared you. Something has come close to shutting you down. So you're searching for these answers, some reason or logic to make you not afraid. But guess what? Death is terrifying. You can't change that. Death is unpredictable and unknown. Always has been. So while you're searching for answers that might not even exist, you're missing out on life!

Therese
At least I'm here!

Daniel
Here?

Therese

At least I'm living. A lot of people just give up. I'm still alive.

Daniel

Are you? Holed up with a typewriter? Overwhelmed by everything. That's being alive? Maybe suicide is a better option.

Therese

I would never hold onto death the way you do. Never accept it!

Daniel
Acceptance is failure?

Therese
Death is failure!

Therese stands, distraught. Daniel stands, angry. Both are relentless.

Daniel
That's where you're wrong! Success stories, survival stories aren't just made from miracles! I'm a success by fighting!

Therese
Fighting? Doesn't sound like fighting to me. I thought you were an activist?

Daniel
I am!

Therese
Then why accept it? I will never accept death until I've fully experienced life. Why accept something I'm not ready for?

Daniel
Because death waits for no one. It makes the decisions. You have to face the fact that you are searching for a very large answer – you might just die before you get it!

Therese
I won't stop searching long enough to be buried! I would never just give up and say, "All right. I can die now." I would fight!

Daniel
And I don't? You think I don't fight?! Every day I fight.
Your deepest poems about struggle, terror, loss? Nothing compares to any moment of my life! I fight just to get up in the morning and look in the mirror. Maybe today will be the day I'm gone. That there's no more of me left, stolen while I slept. Are my eyes still bright? Cheeks flush? Am I sure it's not just another

fever?

I fight to stay strong and proud, when my own body is the enemy! I watch people ignore the facts about this disease that doesn't care who it kills – or how cruelly it kills.

I watch my friends die. Some of them – too many of them! – stripped of everything they were, everything they could be, because they trusted the wrong person or shot up with the wrong needle. Because I dared to walk down the street alone and couldn't scream loud enough or fight hard enough to make him stop!

Long pause. Daniel's strength and pride reflected in her body. Therese is shocked, but calm in her own strengths as well.

Daniel
People use the term "innocent victim" for those who contracted AIDS through no fault of their own. But we're all innocent victims. None of us went out and decided, "Oh, I think I'll get AIDS today. I think, I'll take a few decades off my life."

Once I heard a woman talking outside the women's center. She was explaining how real lesbians don't get AIDS, because real lesbians never use drugs and never sleep with men – as if the most common means of transmission were the *only* means. I asked her what planet she was from.

Every day, Therese, every single day there's something different.

I watch our community divide into categories. Fringe, Mainstream. The two factions go on talkshows together and show the world how unorganized we are... how much internal bigotry we've adopted. Meanwhile, as we attack each other, adding our victories to the far-right's, we continue to die. Of AIDS, of bashings, of anti-gay laws that make us criminals.

That is the truth I wake up knowing everyday. That is the reality I face. All that and the fact that my immune system gets weaker–

Daniel puts a hand to her heart and pounds out the rhythmic beat.

<u>Daniel</u>
With every... passing... heartbeat, it gets weaker.

And then, there are the days I'm looking good. The days when I have my energy and I feel strong. That's when people say, "Oh Daniel, you look too good to be sick! You'll be fine!"

Nothing hurts more than that. Those lies. The fact that they can't take the truth, my truth, so they invalidate it – invalidate me!

You watched your father die, Therese, so you know what death is. But I watch friends die and see myself mirrored in their eyes. I watch and know that someday – sooner rather than later – I'll die too, and probably just as painfully as a lot of them.

But I do fight. I have not given up. Despite the truth, despite the fear, I still face every day. I enjoy working with my hands, talking with my friends, feeling the wind! I laugh. I tell jokes. I watch the world, the good and the bad. I do my part to make it a little better.

I wear my red ribbon, not because I'm a star or I'm trying to be chic. I wear it to reclaim me. I'm making it what it's meant to be. A reminder. A promise. I wear it because not a day should pass that we all don't remember. We have no right to forget. Because people are dying. Gays, straights, lesbians, children. We can't forget for a minute. And for those who try, I'll remind them.

I don't have time to sit, controlled by my fears, or ride a rollercoaster of overwhelming despair. I do not close my eyes to reality or cover my ears to the truth. I accept death without any answers from life.

So, yes, I am dying, Therese. But I'm living a hell of a lot more than you are!

Daniel pauses. Continues with soft conviction.

Daniel

Life and death are not opposites. They are part of each other. You said that yourself. But they actually aren't mutually exclusive and they don't answer for each other.

Every time you get too close to death, you don't know why you're alive, so you shut down. But life is more than having a beating heart. You have to earn it. To find answers, you can't just sit and think. You have to live. Live even in the face of fear.

I'm not giving some dark and maniacal power called "death" strength, when I say that I'm dying. I'm embracing it!

Therese
Embracing death?

Daniel
My parents didn't do much right, but they gave me a good name.

Therese
Daniel.

Daniel
Like Daniel in the lion's den. When he was faced with death, he discovered how powerful faith could be. And an angel was sent to be with him....

Therese
I remember the story.

Daniel
Do you know what your name means? The harvest and the reaper. Beginning and end. Life and death.

Therese
Both?

Daniel
They aren't mutually exclusive.

Therese
I suppose something can't answer questions about itself?

Daniel
Death has given me a freedom I've never had before. A respect for life, an appreciation that I feel in every part of me.

Yes, sometimes I'm angry. Sometimes I question what's fair and unfair, but then I think about all the people who live a hundred years and never know just how fine laughter is, who never feel risk and victory, who never truly live. I've learned not to do anything that doesn't feel true to who I am. To have realistic goals, and always to be proud of myself because I only get one me. You never know when you might not wake up some morning. How would you feel if this were the last day of your life?

Therese
That sounds so dark.

Daniel
Have you ever thought about why you've made that word – darkness – into something so wrong? Genesis says, Creation began in the dark. And from beneath the sea, Evolution began in the dark. Without darkness, you wouldn't know what light is.

I agree with what you said before. We are here for a reason, each of us for something. But maybe the reason for living is to live.

Therese
Look at the waves, Daniel. Which is stronger? The water or the shore?

Daniel
The water. It erodes the shore.

Therese
But if the water is more powerful, then why can't it stop from coming back to the shore again and again? Why can't it stop itself from coming back? It's drawn to the sand and stone. The shore has power over the water.
Life ends in death. Life can't stop itself from ending that way. I want to know what can. What isn't forced to end in death? What isn't compelled to die? I want to know what won't die.

Daniel
Therese, immortality doesn't exist. Nothing lasts for eternity.

Therese
Death does. I want to find something that is just as strong, even stronger, than death.

Pause. Daniel sits and then Therese.

Daniel
You know, if being alive is so great, how come living people complain all the time? When was the last time you heard a dead person complain?

Therese looks at her disbelieving.

Daniel
I always wanted to be stand-up comedian, but my doctor says I won't be standing that long.
Just a little grave-side humor!

Therese
          I can't stand that! You mock your struggle!

                                Daniel
          It makes my life my own! You make me sound so grand.
I'm not a docu-drama. I'm not someone's symbol of suffering.

                                Therese
                           Aren't we all?

                                Daniel
                      Therese, go like this...

          Daniel takes her own wrist between her fingers. Therese
follows suit.

                                Therese
                      What are we doing?

                                Daniel
          Checking for a pulse. Sometimes I forget which one of us
is dying.

          Therese looks at their hands. Therese reaches out to
touch Daniel, but Daniel jerks away. Daniel does not look at
Therese. Therese touches a hand to her own mouth.

                                Therese
                             Daniel?

                                Daniel
                               Hm?

                                Therese
          The angel in the lion's den.... It touched the mouths of the

lions, so they couldn't hurt Daniel.

Daniel
Yes.

Therese
Did the angel touch Daniel? Does anyone?
I want to know why you won't let me touch you. What's
changed? When you kissed me–

Daniel
Momentary insanity. I apologize.

Therese
Sweet insanity. Don't apologize.

They look at each other.

Therese
So now you're sane. You won't let me. Why?

Therese reaches for Daniel. Daniel stands quickly.

Daniel
No one wants to court death.

Therese
I know I shut my eyes and ears sometimes. And what
you're saying – about how maybe I'll never find my answers –
that terrifies me. But you don't. You don't scare me at all. And
no, I don't want to court death. Death isn't what I want. I want
you.

Daniel
You've known me for two days.

Therese
Most lesbians would be living together by now.

Daniel
You said "lesbian."

Therese
I said, I want you.

Daniel
I wish I could believe you.

Therese
Why can't you?

Daniel
Beneath all your fears, Therese, is there really a brave woman?

Therese
Brave? Brave is thinking things through, facing them eye to eye. I'm just telling you how I feel.

I don't think I run from death. I know it too well. I run from life. I feel drowned by it. But I can learn to swim. If being brave is living when you're scared, then I'm as brave as they come.

Daniel, when you die, you don't have to have someone just watch. They – I could hold you. I can hold you now.

Therese stands.

Therese
If I'm not living, Daniel, then you're not loving. Love and death aren't mutually exclusive either.

Therese reaches for Daniel.

<u>Therese</u>
Will you let me?

Daniel wavers, then goes rigid, suddenly angry at herself – at fate – she holds her hand up for Therese to stop.

<u>Daniel</u>
In this lion's den, I never asked for the angel. I was just fine with my faith. Just fine waiting for the lions.

Daniel leaves. Therese keeps her back turned as Daniel moves across the stage. Daniel is hit with a red light and a voice is heard.

<u>Pusher</u>
You need a little pick-me-up, sweet thing? I've got what you need–

Daniel turns on the Pusher. The red light becomes white.

<u>Daniel</u>
Unless you've got a bottle of AZT tucked between your Rock and your Snow, I don't think you can help much. Or maybe you got some way to make me to stop thinking about what's in my blood whenever I lay a hand on another woman, without doping me up so bad I don't know safe from sorry?
No? I didn't think so.

Therese turns and moves to watch Daniel from across the stage. Daniel confiscates the Pusher's money.

Daniel
Quite a wad, guy. Oldest trick in the book to keep your cash down your pants. I see it's been a profitable day for you... until now.

I'm calling the cops when I get to payphone on the corner. Take off now and I promise I won't bleed on ya.

Daniel moves on a few steps and is hit with a green light.

Prostitute
Hey, baby – Daniel?

The green light becomes white.

Daniel
Hey, Hidi, right? You were at the Safer Sex Workshop I taught at the college.

Yeah, I'm doing all right. Still alive, ya know.

Well, not really. I've been working a lot, so dating has kind of fallen to the way side. And it takes a special kind of lady to be with me. Someone not afraid to be... close to the edge.

Daniel almost looks back to Therese and the cafe.

Daniel
Huh? Hey, you take care of yourself too. As a matter of fact, here. Let me share some extra funds that I just, oh, appropriated. Take a few nights off, eh?

But later on, you remember to tell those guys: Either wrap it, or take it home and whack it!

Daniel moves on. White light follows. She bends and mimes waking someone who is laying on the ground.

Daniel
Hey, pal. I saved half my prize money just for you

Daniel kneels.

Daniel
And you know what? I know this place right down the street that's run by some friends of mine.

No, it's not a mission. You pay rent, about a dollar a week, and you have to do your share of chores too. Better than this hard concrete though, I bet.

Yeah, it's a bed and three hot meals a day. I could walk you over, if you want? Sure... come on.

Daniel stands, mimes helping the Panhandler up and off the stage.

Therese
It'll take someone more than special to love you, Daniel O'Donald. More than an angel, I think. They'd have to match your heart.

I don't know if the world is ready for you but I am. I'm willing to try. Will you let me? If we both face our demons.

Lights dim. The spotlight fades last from The Edge Cafe hanging sign. Act Two ends.

Act Three
Words Like Breath

Scene One

Curtain up. Blue light on Therese in her home. She sits before her desk, staring ahead. There is a piece of paper in the typewriter. The crumpled papers and chopped pieces of apple are gone.

The rest of the stage is dark. To one side is the cafe. To the other side is Daniel. She sits on an examination table at the doctor's.

Blue lights show the Television and Radio when their voices are heard.

<u>Therese</u>
Mama... you never were, were you? You never were a mother. Never even tried. Never even gave it a thought. You were never sober long enough.

Therese rises and moves forward to center stage. Blue light becomes white.

<u>Therese</u>
But now you are.

<u>Television</u>
Forty thousand seven hundred-twenty Americans die from alcohol each year. Another four hundred nineteen thousand die from cigarette smoking. Both industries flourish with million dollar advertising champagnes. Imagine if serial killers advertised.

<u>Therese</u>
It's time we talk, Mama. I know it's not something you do very well – listen, I mean. But you're dead. My own captive audience.
I guess I should start at the beginning. I'm your daughter.

Your only child. My name's Therese. Daddy named me. You might remember me when I was a baby... you might not. Maybe even then I embarrassed you.

Radio
Beating a child is a heinous act of violence. Yet hundreds of children each year are brought into hospitals to be treated for abuse received at their parents' hands. But it is the children who are abused with words who keep their scars the longest.

Therese
I never told you a lot of things. I tried when I was little, but I learned pretty quickly that your life was your parties and your next bottle. Learned that if I ever told you something you didn't like, I would regret it. Not with bruises. A battered child would have soiled your perfect image. Not with bruises that showed. So I never told you anything. You never asked. Then it wasn't very long until I didn't want to tell you. Until I wished you weren't even there.

Television
Communication is the foundation of the family unit. Without communication, the family cannot function, cannot relate. The family fails to be a family.

Therese
And I got my wish. You aren't here anymore. So since I'm on a roll, I want another wish. I want you to listen to me. Because I have a lot to say. And you can't interrupt me, or tell me to shut up, or send to my room. You can't even call me stupid – because you're dead and I'm not. I... am... living. Something that you never did.

Radio
The children of the nineties have less respect for their

elders. The adults of the nineties care less about anything but themselves. It is all part of our society's moral and ethical decline.

Therese

I hated the dress you made me wear to Daddy's funeral. You said it was only right that I wear it, all that black silk and lace. But I hated it because it was expensive and fancy, and I was sad.

After the wake that day, when you were passed out on the living room floor, I took that dress and flushed it down the toilet. The plumber was wrong. The pipes didn't burst because of corrosion. They burst because they were full of black silk.

I never told you about Sunday School either. Every week you made me go. You said, it would teach me about God and goodness; I guess at least one of us should have known. You said, it looked right if I went and that people would respect me more. But my teacher told me that Daddy must have died because he was a horrible man. The kids teased me relentlessly, because – you see, Mama – you didn't have a perfect image. You were a drunk, and everyone knew it.

But I did learn something. I listened and learned how so many people become bigots.

Therese's confidence grows stronger as she continues to speak.

Therese

And the dark. I was scared of the dark. But when I asked for a nightlight, you said I was too old.

I was six! I know adults who sleep with a lamp on! I wanted it to be light, so I would know what was around me. So I would know.

Instead, I was surrounded by the unknown every night. I had to constantly wonder. But it taught me how people hate what they don't know, what scares them. How they either hate – or just close their eyes and deny.

And your television set and your damned radio! I couldn't stand them. I couldn't stand the noise they blared when I was trying to write!

Television
Children no longer spend hours a day reading or pursuing hobbies. Television and video games are quickly replacing other activities and pastimes. Video games force children to thrive on stress and competition where players receive points for killing. By age thirteen, a child will have seen ten thousand deaths on television and film.

Therese
I'm a feminist! Even though you swore the world was run by men and that was the way it should be – and that it would never be changed, especially not by women.
Which, by the way, is wrong. The world will be changed. And especially by women!

Radio
Feminist: a woman who fights for the equal rights of all women, no matter what their orientation, color, religion or economic status. One who stands up for herself and her Sisters. A woman who will not be broken.
When a woman is beaten every fifteen seconds, it is essential that every woman be a feminist.

Therese
I'm an environmentalist. Even though you said the Earth didn't matter and the trees weren't so important – that soon all the world would be covered with concrete and it would be a better place when it was.
Which, by the way, is wrong again. The world cannot exist covered with steel and concrete. We either preserve nature or die with it.

Television
Environmentalist: an individual who fights to help keep the planet, its earth, water and skies clean.

When the average family of four would have to plant six acres, each with five thousand trees, to compensate for the amount of pollution they create annually, it is essential that we all be environmentalists.

Therese
Do you remember that young man I went to the senior prom with? The one you liked so much. The one you wanted me to marry? He's gay.

Radio
One out of ten men are gay. One out of ten women are lesbian. There are thirty million gays and lesbians in American today. Thirty million living, loving, having families, sharing their lives – growing stronger. Thirty million. That's a lot of Queers.

Therese
And, Mama, I'm a writer. I've been a writer since Daddy died. I've published six books. Six prose-poetry books. Poems about life and about growing up, about the world and how I see it... even poems about you. You used to say that art was useless. Well, I bought this house with my royalties. My writing helps keep me alive.

And I'm a lesbian. I love women. Do you remember Tessie? She stayed with us for spring break once. She was my first partner. We made love for the first time under your roof... in your bed.

I'm proud to be who I am. Proud to love the way I love. And there's a lot of different ways! I love living with women and talking with them. I love reading books about women, by women and going to their art shows. I love being a lesbian and being part of the lesbian, gay, bisexual, transgendered community.

I love being with a woman and pleasing her – being pleased. Making love with a woman I love, standing by her, being brave with her. These are the most beautiful things I've ever done.

And I know that you probably don't want to hear all this. But that's tough. You need to know who I am. I need you to know that no matter how hard you tried – in your living or in your dying! – you did not break me.

I have survived.

Television

Survivor: one who remains alive or in existence. One who has outlived or outlasted an ordeal, trauma or disaster. Someone strong enough to stand when the storm is through – and when it comes again.

Lights dim from Therese and rise on Daniel who sits on the doctor's table. Daniel is speaking with her new doctor. She begins with uncertainty, then becomes more animated as she becomes more confident.

Daniel

I suppose as my new physician you have a lot of questions. Medical history, lifestyle, beliefs, general attitude. I'll tell you right off: I don't like seeing doctors because I don't want to be touched.

Yeah, I know there's no danger in causal contact. My head understands that, but my fears....

There's a difference between what we're told and what we know. There's a difference between what we're taught and what we learn.

So, let me answer all your questions. And all of my own. When I was still a kid, I knew I was different. I knew that people hated difference, because it wasn't what they knew. And people are afraid of what they don't know. But I knew that I would never let anyone stop me from being me. I was going to make my difference into something powerful – and I did.

My name is Daniel O'Donald. I'm HIV positive. I'm a lesbian. I own my own construction company. I teach Safer Sex Workshops, and I challenge people to open their eyes and *see*. I am strong, loud and proud of who I am. No one and nothing can take this from me.

You see, as gays and lesbians we're told our whole lives what we can't do. We can't hold hands. We can't touch. We can't even love each other. We are told that we're an unfortunate minority and that we deserve the names we're called, the bashings we receive and the prejudice we endure. Sometimes we're told that we don't exist. But we do. In every color, every size, every shape and every age. Whether we are living or dying of AIDS, of cancer – of hatred! – regardless of society's views, regardless even of our own community's views about our health or morality, these views do not limit or govern our hearts and souls. We are still gay or lesbian. We will continue to be.

Now, the first thing I taught myself was that before all else, I am Daniel. I am a human being. The first thing I am is not an activist. The first thing I am is not a lesbian. But, both of these make me who I am today.

I learned that I don't have to be butch or femme, aggressive or submissive. I learned that I don't have to have short hair, wear purple triangles or call myself a dyke. But, if I want to, I can.

I learned that despite what some people try to tell me, I do not have to be closeted. I do not have to be afraid. I do not have to be ashamed... not about anything. I have no reason to be.

When I was growing up, I was told that I'd never amount to anything, because I was a girl. I've had people tell me the same thing because I'm a lesbian.

I laugh at these people! Just standing here – today – is

victory enough. Sometimes, you have to go against what you're told to embrace what you love – to embrace the truth... your own truth. The way I love is right for me. The way I live, the way I die... are mine.

I have fought for the right to walk down the street arm-in-arm with another woman. I have turned the other cheek to prove a point and matched a stranger blow for blow when he attacked a gay friend. Despite the hate, despite the bigotry, despite the discrimination, I am victorious. I will never let anyone stop me from being who I am, loving how I love, living how I choose to live. Nothing can stop me from being Daniel. Nothing. Not even death can erase me. I've touched too many lives.

If I had a wish – just one wish – I wouldn't choose to be cured or even to die gently. I would wish that I could talk – just once – to all my Brothers and Sisters. I would tell them: Don't let anything stop you. Make your difference beautiful. Make your difference powerful. Make it your own. You don't have to be closeted. You don't have to be afraid. You don't have to be ashamed. There's no reason. You have the right to love who you want to love. You have the right to be who you are. You have the right to stand up and be proud.

Turn to the world and say: Ready or not, this is who I am. You cannot change me!

Pause.

<u>Daniel</u>

I'm here today... finally here... because I won't let my own fears change me. I'm not going to be afraid any longer. I'm not.

So, to begin with Doctor, I'd like to shake your hand.

Daniel reaches out her hand as light fades from her and rises on Therese. Blue lights show both the Television and Radio as they speak simultaneously.

Television and Radio
In our world today–

Therese

Shut up! Both of you!

No... actually, go right ahead. You won't control me anymore. You won't exaggerate my anxiety or drown me in despair. I want to hear you. I want to know what's going on in the world. But you will not rule my life again.

Blue lights dim out.

Therese

What's wrong, did I pull your plug? Not much fun when I take your power away, is it?

You know what, Mama? Most of all, I never told you about my searching. About my wanting an answer. All those years, I looked without you knowing. I knew you wouldn't help.

And then you died. You died and I realized I had all these things I'd never gotten to tell you. I never got to tell you... I love you.

I won't forget, Mama, but I do forgive. Because you were living the only way you knew how. Coping, surviving the only way you could after Daddy died. You were so afraid of death, you rushed yourself into it.

I'm not afraid now. I was. I was so afraid of dying without answers. But not anymore.

When you died, it was too much, because our relationship was so incomplete. It was too much like my greatest fear – that I might just die before I've learned what's stronger than death. I was swallowed by doubt. But the tidal wave has receded now, and I don't think it will ever come again. I won't let it. Because there's nothing to fear.

I have my answer. I've found my hope. Her name is

Daniel.

Light fades from Therese and rises on Daniel.

Daniel

Hey, well, I'll think about it. Some of these treatments have done me more harm than good, but who knows, eh? I'll give ya an answer next appointment. Twelve noon prompt. I'll be here or I'll be in heaven!

My change of heart? Facing my fears? Nah, no miracle. I just met an angel.

Mmhm, her name's Therese Weaver. She reminded me what it's all about. Courage. I was afraid so I hated to be touched. But only a coward hates. I decided I better start being brave.

Well, braver!

Daniel takes a paperback from her back pocket.

Daniel

This is one of hers. Just got it today. She's a writer. Lyrical-prose it's called. She's a woman who isn't scared away... not even by death.

Book's called *A Message to the Warriors*. Here, I'll read ya the title piece:

Power. Strength. Courage. Pride. The four commands of a Warrior. In a world where people are so afraid of difference they've made hate a family value and bigotry a blessing, we are in constant need of Warriors. Those who are afraid of nothing – but inaction.

Bigotry, prejudice, censorship, lies and hatred. I knew them and fought them before I was old enough to attend grade school. I know that cowards can hide anywhere and they usually travel in packs under banners of their holy words, repressive politics and segregated morals.

But more than all of this, I have seen those who stand against them. Those who stand for choice, freedom, truth, voice and love. Those who raise their fists, their words and their wills against discrimination. Those who fight fiercely. The Warriors. It is not always easy. It is never easy. But it is needed. Having the power to live, the strength to match blows, the courage to love and the pride to stand up and tell the world–

During this reading, Daniel starts to walk towards the front of the stage. Lights dim behind her. Therese meets her at the edge.

<u>Daniel and Therese</u>
We will not be conquered. We will reach out and find each other. We will be victorious!

Long pause. Daniel turns and moves towards the cafe. Therese hurries to follow.

<u>Therese</u>
Where are you going?

<u>Daniel</u>
To The Edge.

Daniel stops. Therese joins her.

<u>Therese</u>
You stopped.

<u>Daniel</u>
I'm waiting for you.

Daniel extends her hand and slowly Therese takes it. They move on together. As each of the Realties is heard, a blue light touches Daniel and Therese. In the end they stand beneath the white light of the cafe's hanging sign.

Reality 1
More than a million Americans are HIV positive and most of them don't know it.

Daniel
It takes a lot of courage to be tested.

Therese
Even more to do something about the results.

Reality 2
AIDS has claimed more than one hundred eighty-two thousand American lives.

Daniel
The time has come to be brave.

Therese
Cowardice is too costly.

Reality 3
The leading cause of death in America's largest cities for males ages twenty-four to forty-five is AIDS. The AIDS death rate is rising the fastest in young, heterosexual women.

Daniel
AIDS does not discriminate.

Therese
But the world does.

<u>Reality 4</u>
From the playwright Dietz:
>"The disease is omnipresent now. It is no
>longer the wolf at the door. The wolf is in
>the house, at the window, and he's the
>landlord."

<u>Daniel</u>
It is past time that we join together.

<u>Therese</u>
Eviction time.

<u>Reality 5</u>
From the author David Rowan, on theater:
>"We're seeing less people die on
>stage. Now characters are shown living
>with the disease, just as many people do,
>for years."

<u>Daniel</u>
Everyone lives in their own way. Survival is a personal
battle.

<u>Therese</u>
Courage keeps us alive. It is the difference between
existence and survival.

<u>Reality 6</u>
Again from Dietz:
>"These aren't the concerns of a single
>community. It's up to all of us. Writers
>from all different vantage points must
>write about this, because the effects are
>felt throughout our society. We have to

debunk this myth that once we've had one
successful book or movie or play about
something this serious – that it's done. It's
not done."

Daniel touches her red ribbon.

<u>Daniel</u>
It's never done.

<u>Therese</u>
Because we must never forget.

They stand close together.

<u>Daniel</u>
I promise, I won't walk away anymore.

<u>Therese</u>
You waited.

<u>Daniel</u>
I mean before.

<u>Therese</u>
I promise to let you talk about death.

<u>Daniel</u>
Good. Because you can't ignore it. You can't make it go
away or fix me up.

<u>Therese</u>
I know.

Daniel

I don't believe in miracles. I'm not going to get better. You say, you love me, but it can't be under the standard terms. Forever and ever, with the happy ending and the castle on the hill. The ending won't be happy.

You're going to have to look at me, listen to me, and know you won't have me forever. This disease has its own ways. It's own time card. It could be...

Therese

Tomorrow. Next month. Years from now.

Daniel

I live in the moment. No planning ahead for next Christmas. No growing old in matching rocking chairs. We'll never be able to take each other for granted. If we argue, there might not be tomorrow to make up.

That's why forever doesn't work. Not the way people mean it. I think forever should mean, for as long as you want me. Not some infinite number of days. We aren't immortal. Why pretend to be? Why say forever, instead of, for as long as you need me?

I don't have all the answers....

Therese

Just the answers for you.

I've watched you now. At first, I thought you were such a contradiction. But you aren't. So full of strength and energy, such passion for life. But you insist on saying that you're dying of AIDS not living with it.

Daniel

A lot of people say living. It's how they reclaim themselves. How they live. I've claimed the power of death, the freedom. It's part of me. It's not the painful part–

Therese
It's the freedom that gives you courage.

Daniel
I can live because I've taken my control back. Living or dying, I'm always Daniel. My own.

Therese
Not a contradiction. A balance.

Daniel
Yes, a balance.

Therese
That's what I've been searching for. Never running from death, but always shutting down when it got too close. But I've found my balance – my answer.
What can't death end? What lives even when you die? *We've* been searching, Daniel. Searching for the same thing. Love. Love in the face of challenge.

Daniel
Courageous love.

Therese
My mother, she died last month. She became an alcoholic after we lost my father. She... never let me hold her.

Daniel
Freud would have a field day.

Therese
She always denied that love could exist in the face of challenge, so I never knew what I was searching for. Never knew

its name. Until you knocked.
    I thought it was death at the door.

<u>Daniel</u>
It was.

<u>Therese</u>
But more. You're stronger than death. Despite death you're filled with the courage to live, to face the world.
    You're the reason the water keeps coming back to the shore. You showed me my courage... to fall in love with you.

Daniel teases gently.

<u>Daniel</u>
Was it love at first sight, Therese?

<u>Therese</u>
Well, first sight was just a glimpse – two weeks before you used my phone. I looked out my window and you had your jacket caught in a cement mixer.

They laugh and take hands.

<u>Therese</u>
At the edge.

<u>Daniel</u>
That we are.

<u>Therese</u>
The edge between life and death.

<u>Daniel</u>
Known and unknown.

Therese
Before, I was always trying to walk that line. Denying that anything was unknown. Trying to answer every question. But it's not going to happen, is it? If I want answers I just have to live with my eyes open.

Daniel
It's good to have open eyes. People die when the world is blind.

Therese
You've given me so much to see.

Daniel
You've given me someone to see it with.

Therese
Anything, Daniel.

Daniel
Just promise me, don't loose you in loving me.

Therese
Loving you is being me.

Daniel
Not all of you.

Therese
Just the most beautiful part.

Daniel
Can you really walk this path with me? The unknown. Can you live this life moment to moment? Even with the hurt of losing me?

Therese
It will hurt more to lose you, if I never get to love you.

Daniel
Therese... will you hold me?

Therese embraces her.

Therese
For as long as you need me, Daniel. For as long as you need me.

They stand embracing as the light narrows to spot them alone. Daniel's and Therese's pre-recorded voices come over the speakers; their words of hope replace the other foreboding voices.

Therese's Voice
Because living is much more than just a beating heart, and dying is more than a stopped one. Only when we take fear in our hands – when we are faced with death and look it in the eye – have we conquered it. And that is the true victory. That is life.

Daniel's Voice
The time is past due. The time is now. From all walks of life, we must come together. See the light and dark. Face the known and the unknown. Stand at the edge.

Light fades out. Curtain falls.

▽✦▽✦

About the Author

(Photo taken by Cris Newport in 1994 when "At the Edge" was written.)

Born in Seattle, Washington in 1973, Jennifer DiMarco has been writing and publishing since before she could legally drive a car. She is the author of over a dozen novels, stage and screen plays, in addition to several children's books and board games. She insists that this is proof that having lesbian parents has many advantages.

Though she has been employed as a martial arts instructor, a construction worker and a chase-driver, Jennifer is currently the driving force behind Pride Publications where she intends to stay.

In 1997 look for an audio recording and a video production of "At the Edge" as well as live productions of the play throughout Ohio.

To contact Jennifer, or any other Pride author, write to Pride Publications, POB 148, Radnor, Ohio 43066-0148, or email PridePblsh@aol.com.

Pride Publications

bringing light to the shadows
voice to the silence

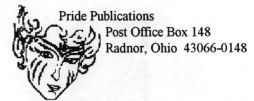

Pride Publications
Post Office Box 148
Radnor, Ohio 43066-0148

Our History

Pride Publications was founded in 1989 by a circle of authors and artists. A publishing house dedicated to shedding light on misconceptions, challenging stereotypes and speaking for those not spoken for. A press created for the authors, artists and readers, not for profit. With several imprints and divisions, Pride publishes books in all genres by all kinds of authors, regardless of gender, orientation, race or age. We are always looking for new projects that others might consider "too wild, too risky, too truthful." At Pride we believe that risk and diversity are part of life. We believe in opening eyes.

Our Facts

Pride Publications works with artists, authors looking for publishers, authors self-publishing who want help, and authors in need of agents. Authors published with Pride receive 10-15% of gross monies received and retain the rights to their book. Authors will also have say in all edits, artwork and promo done for their book.

Authors co-publishing with Pride's help pay only half of the paper costs. Pride pays for all other costs and offers all standard services including accounting, advertising, storage, tour planning, representation and international distribution. Authors receive 50% of all gross monies received.

Authors working with Pride literary agents will receive complete industry representation for 12% of gross royalties received.

Artists working with Pride novels receive advance payment for their art in addition to royalties on all two dozen products that will feature their art. Artists working with Pride children's books receive royalties equal to the author's.

Author submissions: Send complete manuscript, typed, single-sided, double-spaced on white paper. Resume and bio. Summary of entire manuscript. SASE for return of manuscript.

Artist submissions: Send five to ten color and black-and-white samples of artwork. Resume and bio. Cover letter discussing what types of projects you are interested in working on. SASE for response.

Show Your Pride!

Pride Publications offers many products featuring our full-color book covers including tee-shirts ($15.00), mugs ($15.00), canvas tote bags ($18.00), baseball caps ($18.00), 20 x 30 inch posters ($15.00) and 2 1/2 x 3 inch cloth patches ($12.00), great for sewing on jackets or backpacks.

Send check or money order to Pride Publications. Include 10% of your total order for shipping. Please specify size (if necessary) and design desired. Thank you!

Matters of Pride

Books and Plays

The Redemption of Corporal Nolan Giles. Historical Fiction. Jeane Heimberger Candido. A rich, haunting tale set during the Civil War by a talented writer and Civil War enthusiast. The Civil War has never come alive as it does on these pages. Perpare yourself for the truth.

ISBN 1-886383-14-6 $11.95

Annabel and I. Romantic Fantasy. Chris Anne Wolfe. Set on Chautauqua Lake, the tale of a love that transcends all time and all categories. Jenny-wren is from the 1980s but Annabel is from the 1890s. Features thirteen interior artplates by Chris Storm.

ISBN 1-886383-17-0 $10.95

Bitter Thorns. Adult Fairytale. Chris Anne Wolfe. Magical, sensual retelling of Beauty and the Beast with two heroines. *From the Muse Fairytale Series,* #1. Features eight interior artplates by Lupa.

ISBN 1-886383-12-X $10.95

talking drums. Prose Poetry. Jan Bevilacqua. Lush prose-poetry plus. Love, life, sex and empowerment. Exploring gender and butch/femme in our society today. Features fourteen artplates by Kateren Lopez.

ISBN 1-886383-13-8 $9.95

The White Bones of Truth. Science Fiction. Cris Newport. In a future where film stars are owned by the Studio and independence is illegal, revolution brews. A novel of rock 'n' roll, redemption and virtual reality. Features five interior artplates by Pride Publications.

ISBN 1-886383-15-4 $10.95

**Queen's Champion.* Adult Fairytale. Cris Newport. A classic and enticing retelling of Lancelot and Guinevere's love affair and the legend of Lancelot. *From the Muse Fairytale Series,* #2.

ISBN 1-886383-20-0 $11.95

1000 Reasons You Might Think She Is My Lover. Erotica. Angela Costa. Romantic, rowdy, tasty and titillating. A red-hot, pocket-sized collection that will make you laugh, blush... and look for a lover.

ISBN 1-886383-21-9 $9.95

Fall Through the Sky. Science Fiction. Jennifer DiMarco. In this stand-alone sequel to the future-fiction adventure *Escape to the Wind,* Tyger and her gang the Windriders discover incredible secrets and prepare to face the Patriarchy.

ISBN 1-886383-16-2 $12.95

At the Edge. Play. Jennifer DiMarco. You'll laugh out loud. You'll shout hallelujah. Therese Weaver is a poet giving new meaning to the word "melodrama," and Daniel O'Donald is an HIV+ construction worker and activist. When these two women meet, tectonic plates shift. (Second edition, fully revised.)

ISBN 1-886383-11-1 $9.95

Games

These role-playing games are brought to you by RAMPANT Gaming,
Pride's gaming division. Portfolio bound.

Arena Warriors. Battle adventure where you command a fighting team through the challenges of the Great Arena. Play with friends, alone or through a national club!

ISBN 1-886383-04-9 $9.00

Jewel Fighters. Build your fortress, create your fighting force. A game of strategy and skill. Infiltrate your opponent's kingdom and steal his or her Jewel while protecting your own!

ISBN 1-886383-03-0 $9.00

Kingdoms. For everyone who loves or hates chess. Play on a regular chess board, but each piece has new names, powers and abilities. An age-old tradition made new!

ISBN 1-886383-01-4 $9.00

Children's Books

This book is brought to you by Piccolo Pride, Pride's children's division.
Full-color interiors and exteriors.

The Magical Child. Carol DiMarco and Connie Wurm. In the days of castles and kings, dragons and things, there lived a little girl named Angela Marie who was magic but didn't know it... yet!

ISBN 1-886383-19-7 $10.95

Send check or money order to:
Pride Publications
Post Office Box 148
Radnor, Ohio 43066-0148